SHORT WALKS IN ARNSIDE & SILVERDALE

by David Jordan

Low sun and low tide at the Cove (Walk 11)

CONTENTS

Using this guide.. 4
Route summary table 6
Map key.. 7
Introduction... 9
  Walking in Arnside and Silverdale................................ 9
  Special things to see 10
  Bases and places to stay 11
  Travel 11

The walks
  1.   Arnside Park.. 13
  2.   Around Arnside 19
  3.   Arnside Knott... 25
  4.   Sandside, Dallam Tower and Haverbrack 31
  5.   Beetham, Hale Fell and the Fairy Steps 35
  6.   Gait Barrows and Hawes Water 39
  7.   Leighton Moss and Cringlebarrow Wood 45
  8.   Warton Crag 51
  9.   Silverdale to Carnforth 55
  10. Jenny Brown's Point... 63
  11. Arnside Tower from Silverdale 67
  12. The Pepperpot and Eaves Wood 73
  13. Middlebarrow Wood and Eaves Wood............................ 79
  14. Arnside to Silverdale 83
  15. Levens Park and the River Kent 89

Useful information.. 94

USING THIS GUIDE

Routes in this book

In this book you will find a selection of easy or moderate walks suitable for almost everyone, including casual walkers and families with children, or for when you only have a short time to fill. The routes have been carefully chosen to allow you to explore the area and its attractions. Most routes are circular, although some linear walks may be included that use public transport to get back to the start. Although there may be some climbs there is no challenging terrain, but do bear in mind that conditions can sometimes be wet or muddy underfoot. A route summary table is included on page 6 to help you choose the right walk.

Clothing and footwear

You won't need any special equipment to enjoy these walks. The weather in Britain can be changeable, so choose clothing suitable for the season and wear or carry a waterproof jacket. For footwear, comfortable walking boots or trainers with a good grip are best. A small rucksack for drinks, snacks and spare clothing is useful. See www.adventuresmart.uk.

Walk descriptions

At the beginning of each walk you'll find all the information you need:

- start/finish location, with postcode and a what3words address to help you find it
- parking and transport information, estimated walking time, total distance and climb
- details of public toilets available along the route and where you can get refreshments
- a summary of the key highlights of the walk and what you might see

Timings given are the time to complete the walk at a reasonable walking pace. Allow extra time for extended stops or if walking with children.

The route is described in clear, easy-to-follow directions, with each waypoint marked on an accompanying map extract. It's a good idea to read the whole of the route instructions before setting out, so that you know what to expect.

Maps, GPX files and what3words

Extracts from the OS 1:25,000 map accompany each route. GPX files for all the walks in this book are available to download at www.cicerone.co.uk/1158/gpx.

What3words is a free smartphone app which identifies every 3m square of the globe with a unique three-word address, e.g. ///destiny.cafe.sonic. For more information see https://what3words.com/products/what3words-app.

USING THIS GUIDE

Walking with children

Even young children can be surprisingly strong walkers, but every family is different and you may need to adapt the timings given in this book to take that into account. Make sure you go at the pace of the slowest member and choose a walk with an exciting objective in mind, such as a cave, waterfall or picnic spot. Many of the walks can be shortened to suit – suggestions are included at the end of the route description.

Dogs

Sheep or cattle may be found grazing on a number of these walks. Keep dogs under control at all times so that they don't scare or disturb livestock or wildlife. Cattle, particularly cows with calves, may very occasionally pose a risk to walkers with dogs. If you ever feel threatened by cattle, you should let go of your dog's lead and let it run free.

Enjoying the countryside responsibly

Enjoy the countryside and treat it with respect to protect our natural environments. Stick to footpaths and take your litter home with you. When driving, slow down on rural roads and park considerately, or better still use public transport. For more details check out www.gov.uk/countryside-code.

The Countryside Code
Respect everyone
- be considerate to those living in, working in and enjoying the countryside
- leave gates and property as you find them
- do not block access to gateways or driveways when parking
- be nice, say hello, share the space
- follow local signs and keep to marked paths unless wider access is available

Protect the environment
- take your litter home – leave no trace of your visit
- do not light fires and only have BBQs where signs say you can
- always keep dogs under control and in sight
- dog poo – bag it and bin it – any public waste bin will do
- care for nature – do not cause damage or disturbance

Enjoy the outdoors
- check your route and local conditions
- plan your adventure – know what to expect and what you can do
- enjoy your visit, have fun, make a memory

SHORT WALKS IN ARNSIDE AND SILVERDALE

ROUTE SUMMARY TABLE

WALK NAME	START POINT	TIME	DISTANCE
1. Arnside Park	New Barns Bay	2hr	5km (3 miles)
2. Around Arnside	Arnside station	1¼hr	2.5km (1½ miles)
3. Arnside Knott	Arnside Knott car park	2hr	5km (3 miles)
4. Sandside, Dallam Tower and Haverbrack	Sandside Cutting nature reserve	2½hr	6km (3¾ miles)
5. Beetham, Hale Fell and the Fairy Steps	Heron Corn Mill, Beetham	2¾hr	7.5km (4½ miles)
6. Gait Barrows and Hawes Water	Eaves Wood car park	1½hr	3km (1¾ miles)
7. Leighton Moss and Cringlebarrow Wood	RSPB Leighton Moss	3hr	9km (5½ miles)
8. Warton Crag	Warton Crag car park	1¾hr	4km (2½ miles)
9. Silverdale to Carnforth	Silverdale station	3¼hr	9.5km (5¾ miles)
10. Jenny Brown's Point	The Shore, Silverdale	1¾hr	5km (3 miles)
11. Arnside Tower from Silverdale	The Shore, Silverdale	2hr	5.5km (3½ miles)
12. The Pepperpot and Eaves Wood	Eaves Wood car park	1½hr	3km (1¾ miles)
13. Middlebarrow Wood and Eaves Wood	Eaves Wood car park	2¼hr	4.5km (2¾ miles)
14. Arnside to Silverdale	Arnside station	2¾hr	7km (4¼ miles)
15. Levens Park and the River Kent	Levens Bridge	1¾hr	4.5km (2¾ miles)

MAP KEY

HIGHLIGHTS
Coastal views and woods
Getting to know Arnside
Wildlife and spectacular scenery
The River Bela and Dallam Park
Limestone pavement and history
Meadows and wetland
Wildlife and woodland
Heathland, beacon and possibly birds of prey
Historic route across the saltmarsh and a scenic train ride back
Jack Scout, coastal views and Woodwell
Coastal walk and Arnside Tower
Ancient woodland and beech circle
Arnside Tower and woodland
Arnside Knott Wood, Arnside Tower and Silverdale
Ancient parkland, goats and deer

SYMBOLS USED ON ROUTE MAPS

- **S** Start point
- **F** Finish point
- **SF** Start and finish at the same place
- **4 ▶** Waypoint
- ~ Route line
- ~ Alternate route line

MAPPING IS SHOWN AT A SCALE OF 1:25,000

DOWNLOADED THE GPX FILES FOR FREE AT
www.cicerone.co.uk/1158/GPX

The south-west corner of Arnside Knott (Walk 3)

INTRODUCTION

Victorian houses at Arnside (Walks 2 and 14)

One of the smallest Areas of Outstanding Natural Beauty (AONBs) in England, the Arnside and Silverdale peninsula is sometimes overlooked by potential visitors as they drive by on their way to its larger neighbour, the Lake District. For those lucky visitors who do 'discover' it, a real treat is in store. The AONB designation reflects the incredible beauty of its landscape, the diversity of its plantlife and wildlife, and the cultural history that means that in every corner there is a story to be uncovered.

The weather too plays a part in making Arnside and Silverdale what it is. Even when rain lingers on the higher hills of the neighbouring Lake District, it can be clear and sunny here. Additionally, being on the boundary of a north/south climatic divide means a rich diversity of plant life can be found here.

Walking in Arnside and Silverdale

There is a considerable variety of walking in and around Arnside and Silverdale. Paths follow the coast, over crags, through farmland, heath and woodland. A few hills are steep, but not high, and are well within the abilities of most people, and there are plenty of flatter coastal walks on offer. Walks can be easily combined with visits to places of interest such as the RSPB reserve at Leighton Moss, or the Wolf House Gallery in Silverdale. It is easy to see why so many visitors to the area return again and again.

SHORT WALKS IN ARNSIDE AND SILVERDALE

The spectacular coastline where limestone rock meets estuary sand, provides miles of unspoilt walking with often dramatic crags, twisted windswept trees, the occasional cave and, of course, the extensive sky glimmering in the channels of the vast bay. For some people, one of the key attractions is the chance to walk amid the area's semi-ancient woodlands, many of which continue to be managed under traditional practices such as 'coppiced with standards', cattle-grazing, dry-stone walling and hedge laying. On Arnside Knott the rare juniper dates back hundreds of years, and yet it remains low and warped into strange shapes by the nibbling of generations of deer and rabbits. In Eaves Wood the twisted old yews have stood for over 400 years, while the collection of small-leaved limes are in effect all from a single tree as each grows from a dropped branch of a former tree.

Many tracks are old rights of way that have been travelled by local people through the centuries, and the plethora of footpaths are well waymarked. Routes are often good underfoot, but care must be taken on exposed limestone which can become slippery when wet. In areas that are managed for public access, such as Leighton Moss, Eaves Wood, Trowbarrow and Haweswater, some tracks are passable with wheelchairs or pushchairs; however, where paths cross farmland, stiles and narrow stone wall 'step-throughs' are present.

Special things to see

Under the cool canopy of Eaves Wood is the place to be on a hot day, or among the shady limestone crags below the Fairy Steps. Step out to the heathland of Jack Scout and rest in the

Meadow grassland at Gait Barrows nature reserve (Walk 6)

Low tide at Arnside (Walks 2 and 14)

Giant's Seat to watch the sun glimmering across the bay, then drop down to the Cove and explore the cave and look for clues to an industrial past. Leighton Moss and Hawes Water are a haven for birdlife, or take a walk through Dallam Park among the deer. Beetham is idyllic and the Wheatsheaf Inn offers a perfect opportunity to enjoy a refreshing drink, then walk up to the tranquillity of the Heron Corn Mill by the river. Of course, no visit would be complete without 'seaside' fish and chips from Arnside's famous chippy. Perhaps most special of all is that here, you can do much of this on foot.

Bases and places to stay

The villages of Arnside and Silverdale provide the starting point for many of the walks. Accommodation options are plentiful in or close to the villages. The caravan sites at Holgates and Gibraltar Farm in Silverdale are very well placed for walks too, and the friendly scale of the area means that wherever you stay much of what you might choose to visit can be accessed by taking advantage of the walking routes in this guide.

Travel

The train is a great way to get to this area, with the Furness line between Lancaster and Barrow stopping at Carnforth, Silverdale and Arnside before crossing the viaduct to Grange-over-Sands and beyond. Silverdale station is outside of the village but linked to it by the regular number 51 bus. The area is within easy reach of the M6 too. Best of all, the scale of the AONB encourages a stroll, and a walk along the numerous footpaths is by far the best way to explore.

Looking south from the caravan park

WALK 1
Arnside Park

Start/finish	New Barns Bay
Locate	LA9 0BN ///allow.guess.routs
Cafes/pubs	Cafe at New Barns caravan park
Transport	Train to Arnside, followed by 20min walk to New Barns Bay
Parking	Layby outside New Barns caravan park
Toilets	Nearest public toilets on Arnside promenade

Time: 2hr
Distance: 5km (3 miles)
Climb: 150m

A gentle circular walk on good tracks taking in the beautiful coastline, heath, and woodland of Arnside Park

This lovely walk follows coastline and woodland paths to Far Arnside, with far-reaching views over Morecambe Bay. It returns through heathland on the lower slopes of Arnside Knott. Early or late in the day are great times to see deer and rabbits grazing at Heathwaite, and to glimpse the sands glowing in the low sun.

The beach at sunset

1 At the entrance to New Barns caravan park take the beach path right. This is good in all but the highest tides. If you prefer, step up left from the beach at various points, into the trees, to join a good path running parallel. About halfway around White Sands Bay, after **Blackstone Point**, a path leads left through static caravans, into the trees. It is possible to continue around the coast to Far Arnside. However, the coastline path can be narrow and tricky in places.

2 Turn left uphill on gravel to join a park road, which then divides around trees. Take the track on the right here, behind a caravan, and head uphill, keeping left as the path forks. Go through a gate leaving the caravan site, then turn right after a few metres. At a fork keep left and ignoring a later track right, keep ahead. The broad path rises through woodland, before undulating, then descending to meet a boundary wall and a gate.

WALK 1 – ARNSIDE PARK

> ⓘ *The AONB is a haven for wildlife. Over half of the UK's flowering plant species are here, and as many as 34 species of butterfly*

3 Go through the gate to reach a small road at a corner. This is Holgates caravan park. Take the road ahead left, uphill, and continue through the caravan park eventually bearing left to reach the entrance barrier. Beyond this continue along the lane ahead between cottages at **Far Arnside**. After a short distance you will see a gate and squeeze-stile signposted 'Arnside via the Knott'. Cross the stile and proceed up the grassy track between farm fields. At the head of the track, cross a further stone stile to **Hollins Farm**.

4 Turn left before the buildings, signposted 'Arnside', and proceed uphill to reach a wooden gate. Pass through this into the area known as **Heathwaite**. Heathwaite is very much the quiet side of Arnside Knott and keen observers may spot a wealth of wildlife here. Turn right directly after the gate and take the stony track uphill, keeping the boundary wall on your right. Continue to reach a gate in a further boundary wall and beyond

The path to Arnside Knott at Far Arnside

SHORT WALKS IN ARNSIDE AND SILVERDALE

The saltmarsh at New Barns Bay

that a four-way track junction and bench. Turn left along the bridleway signposted 'Arnside' and continue to the next gate.

5 Turn left again signposted towards 'Copridding Wood and New Barns Bay', then proceed downhill through trees. Bear right ignoring a small side track on the left, by a boundary wall. Continue ahead, ignoring further side tracks, across open ground with potential for sunset views across the estuary. Keep left at a fork and continue to descend through trees, passing through a small gate in a stone wall. Keep ahead now to reach a large wooden gate. Pass through a wall gap to the side and follow the path, bordered by wire fence, to reach a metal swing gate. Go through, turn left onto the road, and downhill around the corner to arrive back at New Barns Bay.

Historically saltmarsh was extensively grazed by sheep and there has been a long history of cutting turf for fuel. Now the shifting channels of the estuary are eroding the saltmarsh at New Barns, an important habitat for a range of species.

– To shorten

Take the footpath through New Barns caravan park instead of the coast path. This is easier walking and shortens the walk by about 15min. Turn left to rejoin the route where the road divides around trees, as mentioned in Waypoint 2.

Morecambe Bay

The spectacular scale of Morecambe Bay lends a sense of grandeur to the surrounding landscapes of woodland, grassland and limestone escarpments. Low craggy cliffs and saltmarshes knit these together with glittering mudflats, sandbanks and tidal islands. Fed by the estuaries of the Leven, Kent, Lune and Wyre, together with other smaller rivers such as the Keer, the bay is riven with low-water channel systems and has an impressive spring tidal range of 9m.

Morecambe Bay is the largest single area of continuous intertidal mudflats and sandflats in the UK, supporting the third largest number of wintering wildfowl in Britain, alongside dense invertebrate communities including exceptionally large beds of mussels.

Looking out across the bay

Great views above the gardens and rooftops of the village

WALK 2
Around Arnside

Start/finish	Arnside railway station
Locate	LA5 0HG ///deriving.drummers.peroxide
Cafes/pubs	Cafes and pubs in Arnside
Transport	Take B5282 from Milnthorpe. Train from Carnforth or Silverdale
Parking	On roadside along the promenade or foreshore car park
Toilets	On promenade

A gentle walk on pavement and tracks with a small climb from the beach to the woods, this route from Arnside station meanders along the promenade and estuary front to the quintessential beach hut ice-cream bar, then returns through the historic woodlands at Ashmeadow, and the quiet passages above this picturesque coastal village.

Time: 1¼hr
Distance: 2.5km (1½ miles)
Climb: 45m

An easy circular meander with opportunities for ice-cream, fish and chips and getting to know Arnside

The beach path

SHORT WALKS IN ARNSIDE AND SILVERDALE

1 Leaving the station, turn right and follow the road to the corner, past Arnside's famous fish and chip shop. Cross to the foreshore car park and take the path along the embankment for a great view of the viaduct. Constructed in 1856 with a single track, the 51-span viaduct was soon extended to take two tracks in 1863. Rejoin the road opposite Ye Olde Fighting Cocks pub, turn right and follow the promenade, first to the pier, then continue past the clock and boat slip. You can drop onto the foreshore at this point, although the upper path continues for some way enabling dry feet even at high tide. Continue to reach the coastguard hut and behind it the Arnside Beach Hut snack bar, where a pause for ice-cream is obligatory.

The pier was built in 1860 as a concession after the viaduct was built, in recognition of the limitations it would place on river trade upstream. It was destroyed by a storm in 1984 and subsequently rebuilt.

2 Leaving the shore now, climb the gravel track to the left of the Beach Hut, ascending through trees then taking a smaller path left at a fork into Ashmeadow Woodland. Climb past a bench with a view of the viaduct, round a hairpin in the track, and join the upper track. Turn left along the terrace, passing an information board about the **Ashmeadow estate**. Shortly after, pass a gate on the right to the old walled garden, now maintained

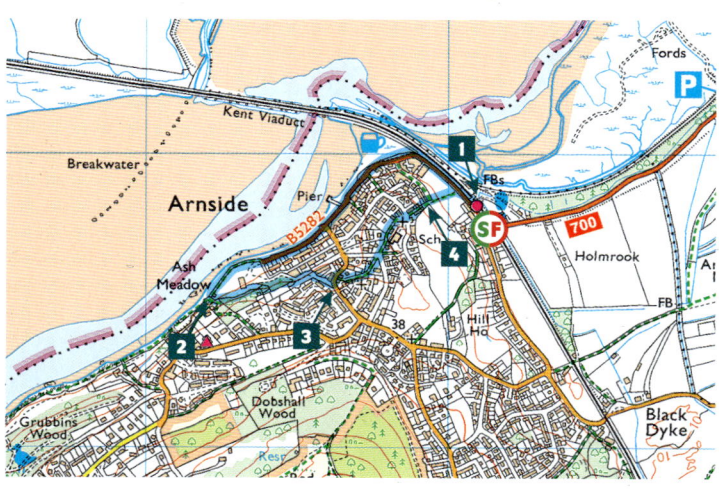

The pier at Arnside

as a wildflower meadow. Follow the path ahead, eventually bearing right, to emerge through a swing gate onto Silverdale Road. If refreshments are needed there is a mini market a short way up the hill to your right.

> Built around 1815, Ashmeadow House became part of Earnseat School for Boys in 1918 and provided education for the next 60 years. The main house was sold in the early 1990s, but the woodlands, walled garden and orchards are managed by a trust for the enjoyment of all.

3 Cross the road and descend left around the corner to Chapel Lane. Turn right and follow this quiet route above the main village. Fork left on a narrow path opposite Arnside Methodist Church, then descend to a road. Cross, then climb again ahead along a narrow, walled path past a folly of unknown origin. Pass St James' parish church on your right then cross Church Hill and take the path ahead known as 'Church View'.

4 Where the houses end, follow the path ahead and descend to the main road, with a fabulous view over the station towards the head of estuary where the rivers Bela and Kent flow out. At the main road turn right then cross the road left to return to the station.

The Albion is a popular place to unwind or watch the sunset

✚ To lengthen

Continue along the coast from the coastguard hut for an out-and-back extension to the saltmarsh at New Barns Bay, where the Bob-In Cafe and playground can be found at the caravan park.

Arnside Bore

One of Arnside's more unusual sights is the Arnside Bore, a tidal wave that can be seen as the tide rushes in across the sands, travelling at up to 16kmph. As the bay narrows the height of the bore can increase, depending on the tides and the season, sometimes rising up to 40cm by the time it reaches the viaduct. Morecambe Bay has deep channels and quicksands that change position daily, which makes venturing out onto the sands dangerous. The King's Guide to the Sands is the royally appointed guide to the ancient crossing of the bay and leads several guided walks a year.

Sunset is the best time to enjoy Arnside

SHORT WALKS IN ARNSIDE AND SILVERDALE

The estuary and viaduct from Arnside Knott

WALK 3
Arnside Knott

Start/finish	*Arnside Knott National Trust car park*
Locate	*LA5 0BP ///crescendo.worked.stiletto*
Cafes/pubs	*In Arnside*
Transport	*Train to Arnside followed by 30min walk*
Parking	*Arnside Knott National Trust car park (free)*
Toilets	*Nearest public toilets on Arnside promenade*

Time: 2hr
Distance: 5km (3 miles)
Climb: 160m

A moderate walk with a rewarding climb up Arnside Knott for stunning views in every direction

A highlight of any visit to the area, a walk to the top of Arnside Knott requires a bit of effort for a lot of reward. The climb is achieved early and is followed by more gently undulating paths and tracks. The panoramic views extend over the estuary to the Lakeland Fells and out over Morecambe Bay.

Looking north up the Kent estuary

SHORT WALKS IN ARNSIDE AND SILVERDALE

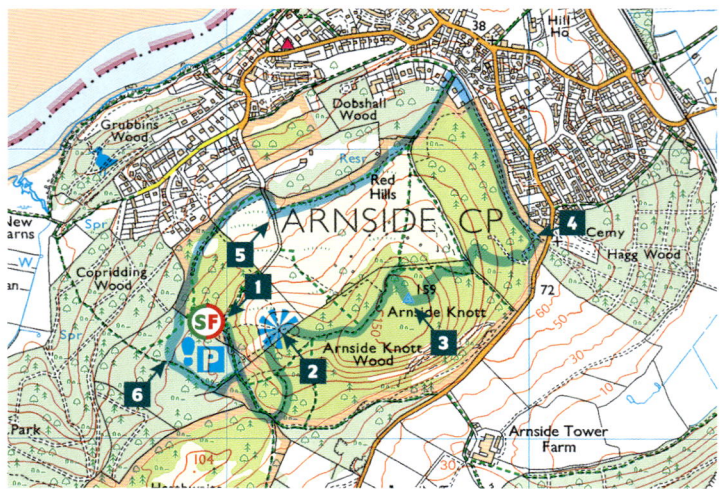

1 From the road into the car park, keep left on a broad track to reach a wide gate. Go through this and the subsequent gate. At a junction by a bench, turn left uphill on a gravel track. Leave the track to the left at a National Trust marker post and go through a small gate before climbing to a viewpoint.

A panorama etching at the viewpoint identifies the Lakeland Fells. Across the Kent estuary the small town of Grange-over-Sands nestles amongst trees, and to the south the full expanse of the bay opens up, with views as far as Heysham.

2 Continue uphill under trees, through a boundary wall. At a fork bear left uphill on a broad gravel track. Proceed to the open top where a bench is provided to enjoy the view. Continue across the top to reach a small gate for a view towards the head of the estuary, then backtrack a little and take the left path uphill to reach the summit trig point.

3 A few metres after the trig point, leave the National Trust marked trail and take the path to the left by a yew tree, with views north to the head of the estuary and the Howgill fells. Follow the path down the hillside, bearing left past old yew trees, to a path junction. Turn right downhill to reach a stone boundary wall, then left to two swing gates. For the shortened

The viewpoint on Arnside Knott

route, keep ahead through the left gate. Take the right gate downhill through trees signposted to Redhills Wood. At a four-way junction turn right. Keep ahead over a forestry track then rejoin it further down, bearing left to reach a larger track.

4 Turn left away from the road and follow the level track for around 10min to reach a gate. Go through, and along the road for a short way, then through a metal gate on your left into Redhills Wood. Climb to a gate at the edge of the trees and go through, then bear right, uphill initially then level and broadly parallel with the boundary wall on your right. Continue across the open, wildflower-rich pasture of Red Hills to reach a gate onto a road.

5 Turn right down Knott Lane, then left after 50m through another gate signed to Copridding Wood. Go across the flank of the hill and through a further gate, then continue ahead, ignoring the side path right. Under trees at a fence take the gap and up a short steep slope to a boundary wall. Go through this gate to a more open area and keep left as the path forks.

6 Merge left onto a larger track and continue uphill to a boundary wall, then left to a track crossroads. From here retrace your steps back to the car park.

Handmade gate on Arnside Knott

WALK 3 – ARNSIDE KNOTT

− To shorten
At the swing gates in Waypoint 3 take the left-hand gate and follow the path parallel to the wall to rejoin the main route across the pastures in Waypoint 4.

+ To lengthen
For a 10min out-and-back extension follow the National Trust marker posts ahead from the summit trig point to a clearing with a small bench for lovely views south and east over Arnside Tower, Silverdale and beyond.

Arnside Knott

At 159m high, Arnside Knott is made up of limestone grassland, woodland, meadow, scree and scrub. The landscape is the product of careful management practices and selective cattle-grazing, making the Knott of national importance for wildlife and home to a rich variety of butterflies, rare wood ants, and some rare and beautiful wildflowers. The 260-acre site has been owned by the National Trust since 1929, along with the adjoining reserves of Red Hills and Heathwaite. In 2005 the Knott was added to the list of 'Marilyns' (UK peaks with a prominence of 150m or more), becoming the lowest Marilyn in England.

Grazed heathland, a diverse habitat

Return through the peaceful village of Storth

WALK 4
Sandside, Dallam Tower and Haverbrack

Start/finish	Sandside Cutting nature reserve
Locate	LA7 7HX ///helper.shuttling.risen
Cafes/pubs	Refreshments at Storth village shop
Transport	Train to Arnside, followed by 30min walk along old railway embankment. Bus 99 (Sunny Ridge stop – school days/times only)
Parking	On estuary roadside at Sandside
Toilets	No public toilets available

Time: 2½hr
Distance: 6km (3¾ miles)
Climb: 110m

Explore the landscape of the upper Kent estuary on this moderate walk, finding clues to a more industrial past

This walk traces the route of the former Arnside–Kendal railway, now a nature reserve, past old limekilns, a shipping warehouse and quarry that hint at Sandside's history. Follow the River Bela to Dallam Tower and return through woodland and the village of Storth.

Parking is free along the estuary at Sandside

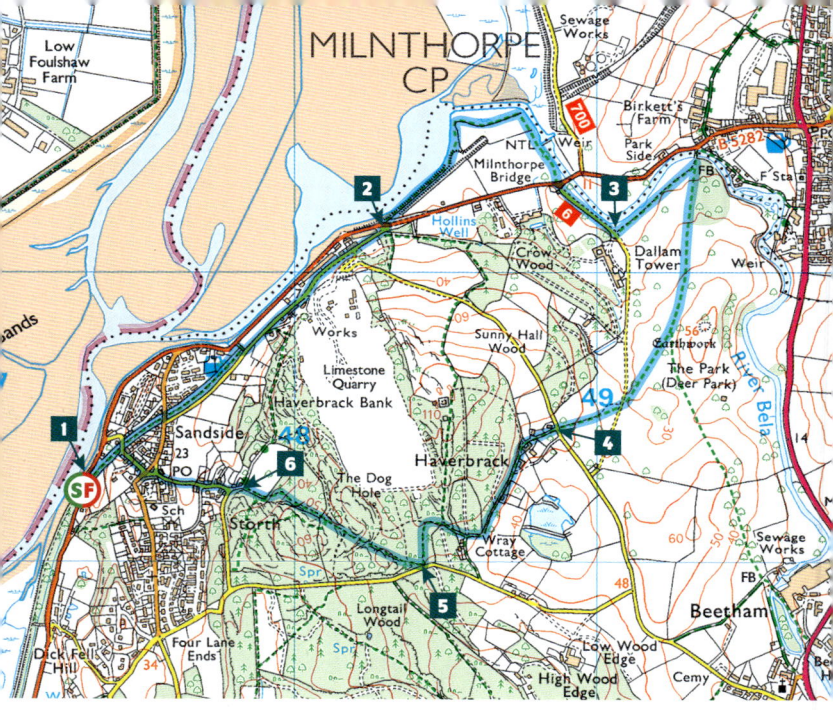

1 With the estuary on your right walk to the end of the pavement, then cross the road and go carefully uphill a short way and through the gate left into Sandside Cutting nature reserve. Turn left and follow the path of the former railway under two bridges. At the far gate turn right, then left onto Quarry Lane, watching out for trucks that access the yards here, then on past the old shipping warehouse on the right and former Sandside limekilns. Continue to the main road, passing the **quarry** entrance. For the shortened route take a right here.

2 At the junction cross the road with care and take the footpath ahead, down steps and along an embankment. Cross a stile, then go through a small gate on the left, down the slipway. Keep right past a lifebuoy to a small gate. Go through and across this field, turning right at the **River Bela**. Keep ahead now towards the

> ⓘ *In 1901 the Northern Quarries Company began operating Sandside Quarry producing lumpstone, railway ballast and agricultural lime*

WALK 4 – SANDSIDE, DALLAM TOWER AND HAVERBRACK

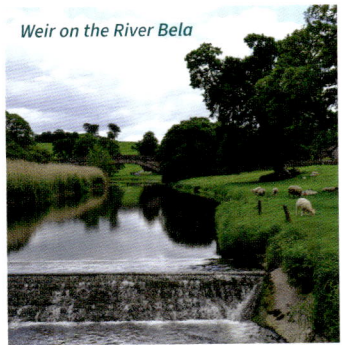

Weir on the River Bela

stone bridge and go through a gate onto the road. Cross the road into **Dallam Park** and soon come to a tall swing gate on your left.

3 Turn left through the gate and follow marker posts across the park around the curve of the river, to reach the stone footbridge that gives access to the small market town of Milnthorpe. This was the original bridge across the Bela and the main route for horse and foot traffic between Milnthorpe and Storth before the road. Do not cross the bridge, but turn right and follow marker posts uphill, enjoying the view across to **Dallam Tower** country house on the right. After the crest, descend to a stone marker cairn. Fork right and further posts guide you to a gate in the fence. Cross the road and go through a gate, climbing slightly left to small gate atop a stone stile.

Until 1942 this was the route of the Arnside–Kendal railway. During WW1 the 'Kendal Tommy' train carried munitions from Barrow, and Arnside viaduct was reinforced to carry the weight of the bomb-laden trains. The route became known as 'The Lifeline of Britain'.

While Dallam may not look like a tower, it is the site of a 15th-century pele tower. The tower was in ruins by the reign of Henry VIII and was replaced by a manor house that pre-dates the early 18th-century building seen today.

Dallam Tower

4 Cross the stile into Haverbrack Lane, and continue ahead, past a cottage and farm. After a few minutes the lane bends to the right. Just as it bends left again take the smaller track right signposted 'Cockshot Lane'. Cross a stile and continue into Burntbarrow Plantation. At a fork keep left, signposted 'Public Road'. Marker posts guide you downhill through trees, to a boundary wall.

5 Take the path right before the wall, to a fork and marker post. Go left now and stay on this track as it rises then descends, eventually reaching the corner of a stone wall at the edge of the wood. Take the gap in the wall onto a narrow path to reach Yans Lane in **Storth**.

6 Turn left then fork right, remaining on Yans Lane. At the third junction, fork left, passing Storth village shop and post office. Cross the road ahead past the WW1 memorial monument, into Green Lane and downhill over the railway bridge, bearing right then left to finish at the estuary.

– To shorten

From the quarry entrance take the lane steeply uphill then the footpath right, up through Haverbrack Woods and downhill to join the main route at the fork in Waypoint 4.

Sandside's industrial past

As you pass the few houses and yards that make up Sandside, you could be forgiven for not realising its significance. From Elizabethan times Sandside was an important hub of trade and industry. This was Westmorland's only sea port, known as the Port of Milnthorpe. Ships were beached on the incoming tide, propped up by staves, and unloaded or loaded before the returning tide. Salt, flour, coal and wine were brought in and limestone from the quarry was shipped out, along with gunpowder from nearby Sedgwick, woollen and cloth goods from Kendal, and iron ore. The building of Arnside viaduct in 1857 and subsequent development of the Hincaster branch of the Furness railway spelled the end of shipping and the port at Sandside.

WALK 5
Beetham, Hale Fell and the Fairy Steps

Start/finish	*Heron Corn Mill, Beetham*
Locate	*LA7 7PQ ///paddocks.broom.marine*
Cafes/pubs	*Pub and tea room at Beetham*
Transport	*Take A6 from Milnthorpe or Carnforth. Bus 755 from Carnforth*
Parking	*Heron Corn Mill*
Toilets	*No public toilets available*

This walk, full of interest, explores the limestone pavement and woodland of Hale Fell, then climbs to the Fairy Steps, a natural staircase down a limestone crag. The return is though Haverbrack and Dallam Deer Park.

Time: 2¾hr
Distance: 7.5km (4½miles)
Climb: 170m

This moderate walk explores the unspoilt limestone pavement of Hale Fell and visits the Fairy Steps

The Post Office, shop and tea room is at the heart of Beetham village

Beetham Church

SHORT WALKS IN ARNSIDE AND SILVERDALE

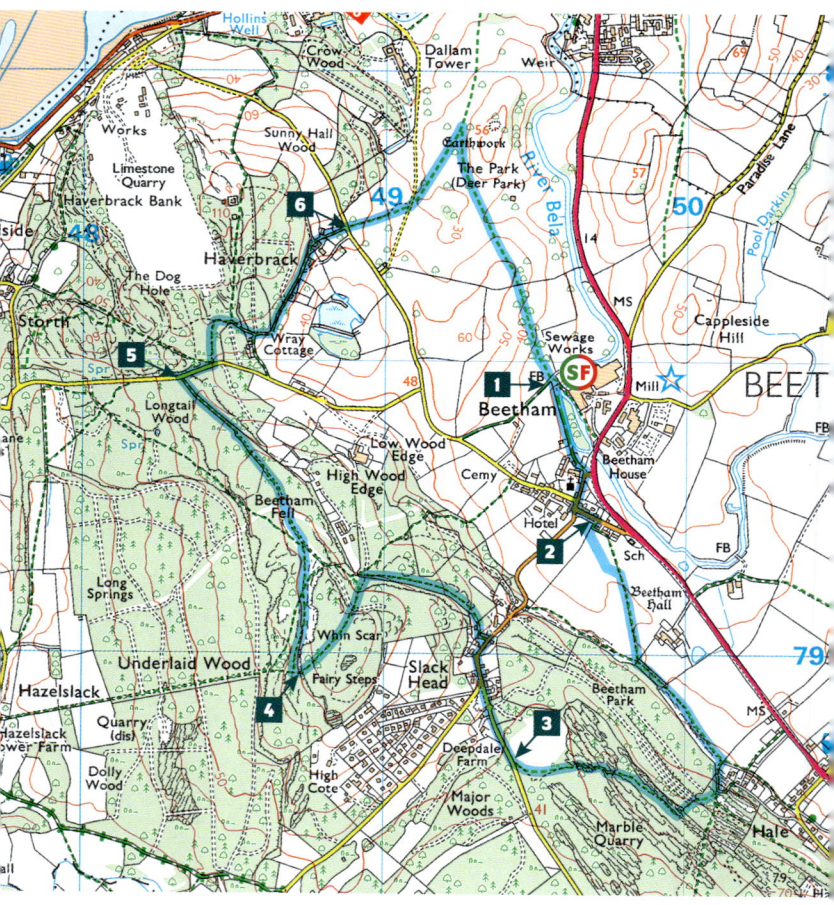

1 From the Grade II listed Corn Mill, take the lane into **Beetham** and right towards the church. Take the gate right to explore the churchyard, exiting by the far gate and then left, past the old post office/tea room back to the road. Pass the Wheatsheaf Inn, dating from 1609, then turn left into Stanley Street. Just before houses on your right is a footpath.

Earl Tostig, brother of King Harold, was Lord of Beetham Manor until 1066, when he was murdered by his brother, shortly before Harold himself was killed at the Battle of Hastings.

2 Follow the footpath across fields towards Hale Fell, with views left to **Beetham Hall**. At the corner cross a stone stile, walk along the boundary wall and over a further stile through a field, rising right to the corner over another stile into woods. At a junction turn right signposted 'Slackhead via Marble Quarry and Limestone Link'. Continue, ignoring side paths, eventually bearing right around a plantation. Marker posts guide you left onto limestone pavement. The limestone is scattered with characteristic deep 'grikes', fissures in which a variety of ferns and sometimes rare wildflowers thrive. Eventually the track rises to meet a small road.

3 Turn right and climb into **Slack Head**. Keep ahead at a junction and go down the road among cottages, to a track on the left signposted 'Fairy Steps'. Take this gently uphill, to a broad stony track. Continue to a stone cairn at a four-way junction. Turn left here and continue as the path becomes enclosed on both sides by wire fencing to reach the open plateau above the **Fairy Steps**. An information board highlights a route left around the steps which you may prefer to take if it's wet.

The earliest buildings of Beetham Hall date from the 13th century

Milnthorpe seen from Dallam Deer Park

Before roads arrived (150–200 years ago), this was the main route to the shop at Beetham for residents of Storth and Arnside. An iron ring in the rock face near the steps held a rope for sacks and parcels to be lowered on the return journey.

4 Squeeze down the steps and at the bottom turn right and follow the track, keeping the crag on your right. Ignore side tracks and continue to meet a stone marker cairn at a four-way junction. Bear left then right, across Beetham Fell, and follow the boundary fence and then the wall all the way down to a stone stile at Cockshot Lane.

5 Cross the road and turn right for a short way, then left at a stone wall gap and straight ahead uphill into the woods. Keep right past a signpost marked 'Haverbrack' and out of the woods, over a stile onto a track.

6 Turn left along Haverbrack Lane to a T-junction and a small gate atop a stone stile. Cross this into **Dallam Park** and head downhill bearing right, following marker posts to a metal gate in the road fence. Cross the road, and subsequent gate following marker posts to a stone cairn. Turn right now and climb the hill, through a wooden swing gate, and downhill between an avenue of beech trees, to reach the car park at Heron Corn Mill.

> **– To shorten**
>
> For a shorter walk of around 1hr 30min, turn right at the Wheatsheaf Inn and walk along the road to the end of the houses, then take a footpath left up the field and into woods, to reach the stone cairn in Waypoint 7.

WALK 6
Gait Barrows and Hawes Water

Start/finish	Eaves Wood car park
Locate	LA5 0QU ///handbook.pigtails.mopped
Cafes/pubs	None on route
Transport	Take Park Road from Silverdale. Bus 51 to The Row. Train to Silverdale station then 15min walk along busy lane
Parking	National Trust car park at Eaves Wood (free)
Toilets	Nearest public toilets in Silverdale village centre or RSPB Leighton Moss visitor centre

Time: 1½hr
Distance: 3km (1¾ miles)
Climb: 30m

Crossing a wildflower meadow, woodland and fen, this gentle circuit is particularly special when early morning mist hangs over the water

Dedicated as a National Nature Reserve in 1977, Gait Barrows is one of Britain's most important limestone landscapes. This route enables a circuit that includes a wonderful wildflower meadow and tracks through woodland around Hawes Water, returning via a leafy lane. It is easy to follow and with little climb, but care must be taken where the footpath crosses stiles and the railway.

The footpath at Gait Barrows reserve is well graded

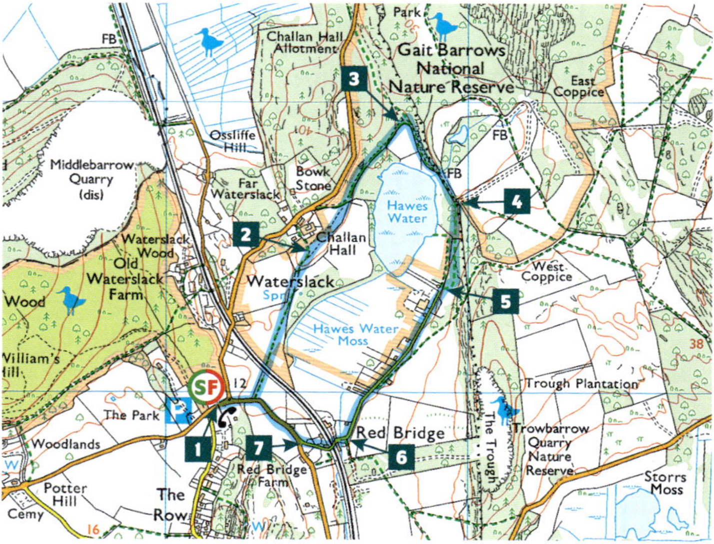

SHORT WALKS IN ARNSIDE AND SILVERDALE

1 Exit the car park and turn left past the bus stop. Cross the road junction and a short way along take the public footpath on the left by a stile, signposted 'Challan Hall'. Cross the stile, keeping the boundary wall on your left until a further stile before the railway line. Cross this and, with great care, the railway track, then over another stile into a meadow and **Gait Barrows** nature reserve by an information board. Follow the worn path across the meadow, where deer often graze, to a swing gate. Pass through and across the continuing meadow towards **Challan Hall**, ignoring the left fork to Waterslack.

The footpath crosses the railway tracks

2 Passing Challan Hall on your left, Haweswater comes into view ahead right, and a series of small marker posts guide you across the meadow where grazing has rendered the footpath less distinct. Pass through the

WALK 6 – GAIT BARROWS AND HAWES WATER

Wildflower meadow and old oaks

boundary wall, signposted 'Public bridleway', and turn right onto a well-surfaced, broad track that leads past **Hawes Water.** The old summer house, now restored as a hide, is a great place to rest and observe the wildlife. Continue to reach a track junction and signpost.

> ⓘ *With no rivers or streams flowing in, Hawes Water is not a lake but a true natural pond*

3 Keep right, marked 'Hawes Water and Moss Lane', between stone walls and follow the perimeter of the lake across a boardwalk where a bench provides another opportunity to enjoy the landscape.

4 Pass through the gate beyond the boardwalk and keep ahead, ignoring the track left. Cross an open stretch, pass through a double gate, then keep left.

5 A final gate beside an information board marks the boundary of the reserve. Keep ahead into the quiet lane, passing a cottage on your right, followed by Hawes Villa Farm and campsite. The lane, bordered by dense hedgerows, passes further cottages, with views to Middlebarrow Quarry on your right.

6 Continue around a sharp right-hand bend and follow the road as it climbs over the railway line, to the road junction.

7 Turn right and take care as you walk along the narrow road, past your outgoing footpath, and on across the road junction to arrive back at Eaves Wood car park.

Leave Gait Barrows nature reserve at Moss Lane

WALK 6 – GAIT BARROWS AND HAWES WATER

– To shorten

For a 30min out-and-back route, all on good tracks and avoiding stiles, park at a layby by Challan Hall and walk as far as Waypoint 5. This would enable wheelchair or pushchair access.

+ To lengthen

At Waypoint 3 take the footpath left signposted 'Challan Hall Allotments'. Turn right at the road, then right again to re-enter the reserve and follow that footpath until a further right enables you to rejoin the main route at Waypoint 4. This will add around 45min.

A rare habitat

The old summer house and Hawes Water

One of Britain's most important areas of limestone landscape, Gait Barrows combines limestone pavement and grassland with woodland and fen and is home to a rich variety of rare wildlife. The rarest of all British wildflowers, the lady's-slipper orchid (once believed extinct) now thrives here alongside Duke of Burgundy and High Brown Fritillary butterflies. The restored reed beds of Hawes Water Moss are home to marsh harrier, bittern and reed bunting.

Secluded waterways are home to native eels as well as birdlife

WALK 7
Leighton Moss and Cringlebarrow Wood

Start/finish	*RSPB Leighton Moss*
Locate	*LA5 0SW ///blazers.tips.duties*
Cafes/pubs	*Cafe at RSPB visitor centre*
Transport	*Train to Silverdale. Bus 51 to station*
Parking	*RSPB visitor centre, or space for 3–4 cars in layby close to bridleway*
Toilets	*RSPB visitor centre*

Rich in natural landscapes, this longer walk explores quiet tracks through wildlife-rich woodland, across meadows and through fields. Good tracks take you across Leighton Moss to Leighton Hall Home Farm, followed by a small climb through Cringlebarrow Wood. Views across Hawes Water can be had on the return, before an excursion around the fascinating Trowbarrow Quarry nature reserve.

Time: 3hr
Distance: 9km (5½ miles)
Climb: 180m

This circuit brings together two nature reserves, with views across a third, via woodland and wildflower meadows

Visitor centre at RSPB Leighton Moss

SHORT WALKS IN ARNSIDE AND SILVERDALE

1 From the car park, turn left and along the road for a couple of minutes, reaching a bridleway on the right marked 'No through road'. Turn right and follow the bridleway ahead. Beyond the reserve continue between farm buildings and cottages, along a tree-lined lane.

2 At **Leighton Hall Home Farm**, leave the lane on a footpath left signposted 'Yealand Redmayne'. Follow the stone wall initially, before veering left to reach a gate. Continue through and across this field to enter the woods. Follow the path rising ahead, bear left joining a vehicle tread

WALK 7 – LEIGHTON MOSS AND CRINGLEBARROW WOOD

Causeway across Leighton Moss

momentarily then right, following yellow waymarks. At a track junction you can detour right to visit Deepdale Pond.

Deepdale Pond was once a beautiful, secluded pond in the heart of a woodland glade. Sadly, a nearby munitions factory explosion in 1917 shook the ground so hard a fissure opened and most of the water vanished, leaving a marshy reed bed.

3 Continue uphill to a junction. Turn left, signposted 'Round Top and Yealand Storrs'.

4 At the next junction turn right to descend, eventually reaching a gate and fenced section, before emerging at Silverdale Road. Turn left through

ⓘ The estuary, once narrower and deeper, is gradually infilling with sediment, and areas such as Leighton Moss are increasingly at risk of flooding

Yealand Storrs. Bear right out of the village then at a forked junction take the footpath signposted 'Moss Lane and Hawes Water', almost hidden between the two roads.

5 This broad track through **Yealand Hall Allotment** passes an area of prominent limestone pavement. Continue until the vista opens on your left to reveal Hawes Water. Take the stile left here and cross the meadow diagonally until you reach the far wall and entrance to Gait Barrows nature reserve, but don't enter.

6 Turn left and take the Moss Lane footpath, following the boundary wall through a gate into woodland. Keep on the path through dappled shade, and through a further gate into a lower meadow, descending diagonally to reach a small gate beside farm sheds, onto Moss Lane. Turn left and follow the lane until a right bend. Take a footpath on the left, signposted 'Trowbarrow Nature Reserve'.

7 Beyond the gate follow a waymark left uphill through woodland to a junction. Turn left and continue into **Trowbarrow Quarry**.

At the centre of the former limestone quarry is an enormous stone known as the 'Shelter Stone'. Tradition has it that men sheltered there when the quarry walls were blasted.

8 After a circuit of the unique quarry environment, whose sheer walls now attract climbers as readily as nesting birds, walk to the quarry end, then turn right to find the information board beside a path through an unusual gate, dedicated to a local climber. Continue ahead to rejoin the road and turn right to return to the start.

> ⓘ *Limestone rock quarried here was fired in limekilns at a constant heat to break down and extract lime powder for building or agricultural use*

> **− To shorten**
> Just before Waypoint 2 take the footpath left, across fields to rejoin the route at Yealand Storrs.

Tawny owls can occasionally be spotted roosting in meadow trees before dusk

Trowbarrow Quarry

The Shelter Stone

Trowbarrow Quarry operated from 1857, providing stone for the expansion of the railways throughout the region. Led by the pioneer James Ward, the Northern Quarries Company became recognised internationally for new techniques in the production and laying of tarmacadam roadstone. The quarry closed in 1959 and has since been managed by the AONB as a nature reserve for quiet recreation, with a rich mosaic of wildlife habitats supporting a wide range of plants and animals. The name Trowbarrow is derived from two words, *trow* meaning trough and *barrow*, the Anglo-Saxon word for hill.

The former quarry at Warton Crag

WALK 8
Warton Crag

Start/finish	*Warton Crag nature reserve car park*
Locate	*LA5 9RB ///verse.beaks.scrambles*
Cafes/pubs	*Old School Brewery, Warton*
Transport	*Bus 51 to Warton*
Parking	*Warton Crag or Old School Brewery*
Toilets	*In Warton village by George Washington pub (2min off route)*

Time: 1¾hr
Distance: 4km (2½ miles)
Climb: 175m

This more challenging walk takes you to highest point of the AONB and is a highlight for nature lovers!

At 163m high and lying on the boundary of north/south climatic regions, Warton Crag is home to both Arctic and Mediterranean plants, and regularly hosts nesting peregrines. The initial climb requires a bit of effort and is steep in places, but it offers great views as you reach the higher ground. Tracks are good down to and along Occupation Road, but more careful footing is required between Waypoints 5 and 6.

The 'rocking stones' on Warton Crag

SHORT WALKS IN ARNSIDE AND SILVERDALE

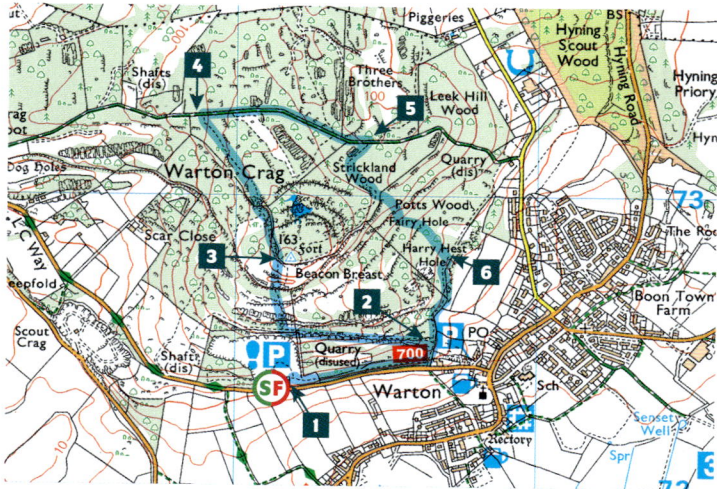

1 Leave the main car park to your rear, turn left and take the footpath parallel to the road, in the direction of **Warton** village, passing a stone carved bench. After 500m bear left uphill and reach a swing gate. If you started from the village or the brewery car park, head uphill on the narrow path at the head of the car park to join the main path here.

2 Pass through the gate and turn left to ascend the crag, climbing gradually, taking care on the limestone while enjoying views across Morecambe Bay and the estuary. Take the gate through a fence, and after 20m find a track on your right, marked with a red/white arrow. Turn right uphill. After a short climb, a side track left will take you on a short out-and-back detour to the 'rocking stones' perched on the edge of the main quarry. Continue to climb, following the red/white arrows, over a V-stile and scramble up a short stony section, keeping left at the top, then follow the path right and on up a well-worn path to the summit of **Warton Crag** with its trig point and beacon.

Approaching the summit, a stone promontory on your left provides unrivalled views across the River Keer estuary and Morecambe Bay. Rising on Docker Moor, near the village of Whittington, the River Keer forms the boundary line between Lancashire and Cumbria.

WALK 8 – WARTON CRAG

The view from Warton Crag extends as far as Heysham

> (i) *The summit of Warton Crag is a Registered Scheduled Monument, the location of a 4000-year-old Iron Age hill fort*

3 Keep left past the beacon, and descend through dense scrub initially, passing an ancient yew tree. Ignore side tracks and continue through a gate, across a track junction, and through open heathland until you reach a boundary wall and gate signposted 'Occupation Road'.

4 Pass through the gate and turn right onto a broad lane. Continue along the lane, ignore the first gate on your right, then as the track rises take the gap in the wall beside the second gate, marked by a signpost and arrow.

5 Follow the stony track uphill, keep left at a fork past a prominent limestone rock, then downhill, taking care on rocks and roots as the descent becomes steeper for a short way. At the foot of this section keep left through two forks, marked by arrows, descending further to reach a track junction.

6 Turn right now, keeping the boundary wall on your left, and follow the path through a side wall, then keep ahead to reach the swing gate and paths to either car park. Turn left

Old School Brewery

through the wall gap to descend to the brewery car park or straight on to follow the path round to the main car park.

Ancient traces

Archaeological finds show evidence of human occupation of Warton Crag as far back as Neolithic times. The remains of a hill fort are just visible at the summit, and it was believed to have been built by the Brigantes (Ancient Britons). The name Warton Crag is derived from Old English *weard* (watch or lookout), *tun* (farmstead) and crag from Celtic *crug* (hill or mound).

− To shorten

Halve the route by turning right at the beacon and walking along the ridge to rejoin the descent route at the second fork in Waypoint 5.

+ To lengthen

At Waypoint 5 continue along Occupation Road almost to its end then turn right through a wall gap and back along the boundary wall at Waypoint 6. This extension is on largely good paths and adds around 15min.

WALK 9
Silverdale to Carnforth

Time: 3¼hr
Distance: 9.5km (5¾ miles)
Climb: 225m

This longer walk is a delightful meander through the lower peninsula, before a 'brief encounter' in Carnforth

Start	*Silverdale railway station*
Locate	*LA5 0SP ///pitching.broadcast.rate*
Finish	*Carnforth railway station*
Cafes/pubs	*Cafes in Silverdale and Carnforth*
Transport	*Train or Bus 51 to Silverdale station*
Parking	*RSPB visitor centre*
Toilets	*Carnforth and Silverdale*

From the woodland at Silverdale Green to the crossing of Quaker's Stang and the heathland of Warton Crag, this route combines some of the best landscapes of the area. Even better is the train ride back, with a view of Leighton Moss that is unrivalled.

The walk starts from Silverdale station

SHORT WALKS IN ARNSIDE AND SILVERDALE

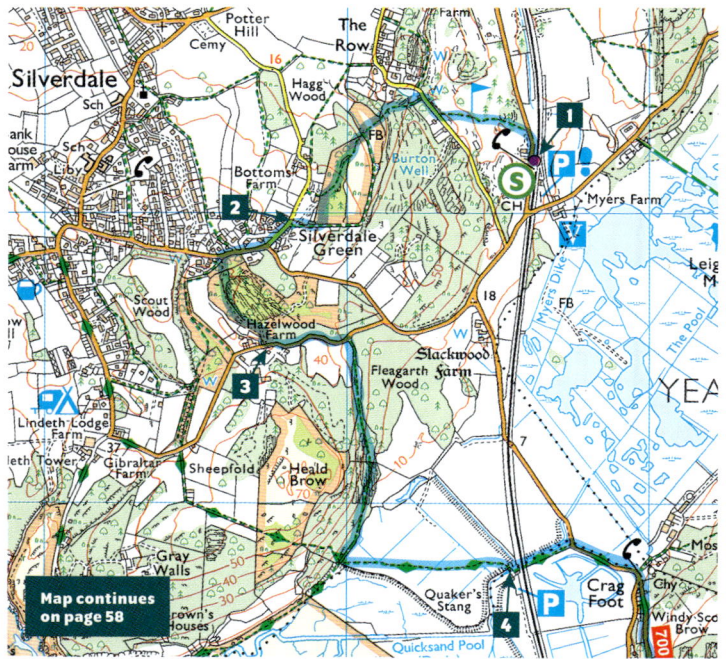

> ⓘ *In 1857 the railway arrived in Silverdale. It was to be routed around the coastline, but influential residents lobbied against this, leaving it over half a mile from the village centre*

1 Turn right from the station then cross the road and take the wall gap on your left, rising to follow markers across the **golf course**. Turn right at the next road for a short way then left along a footpath signposted 'Silverdale'. Descend to a gate, across Lambert's Meadow and a footbridge, then go through another gate and rise through trees to a track. Turn right and out to Bottoms Lane.

2 Turn left, then right onto Stankelt Road. As you reach the end of the trees a track left is signposted 'Pointer Wood'. Take this, crossing open ground and through a gate, onto Hollins Lane.

WALK 9 – SILVERDALE TO CARNFORTH

Quaker's Stang footpath

Footpath descending to Lambert's Meadow

3 Turn left and walk down the quiet road to reach a signpost for 'The Shore & Brown's Point' on your right. Turn right onto the bridleway, narrowing to a path below **Heald Brow**. At a four-way junction turn left, signposted 'Quakers Stang'. Follow the footpath across the embankment to reach a track.

Yealand and Lindeth were home to prominent Quaker families who needed to cross the saltmarsh to meet. Early maps marked a bridge across Quicksand pool as 'Quakers Stang', but the term probably refers to a large stone or series of stone steps used to cross prior to the bridge.

4 Turn left under a railway bridge, and out to the road then turn right. Continue along the road with care, around the corner, past **Crag Foot chimney** on your left, and then take Crag Road uphill. After around 500m reach the bridleway left signposted 'Warton Village'.

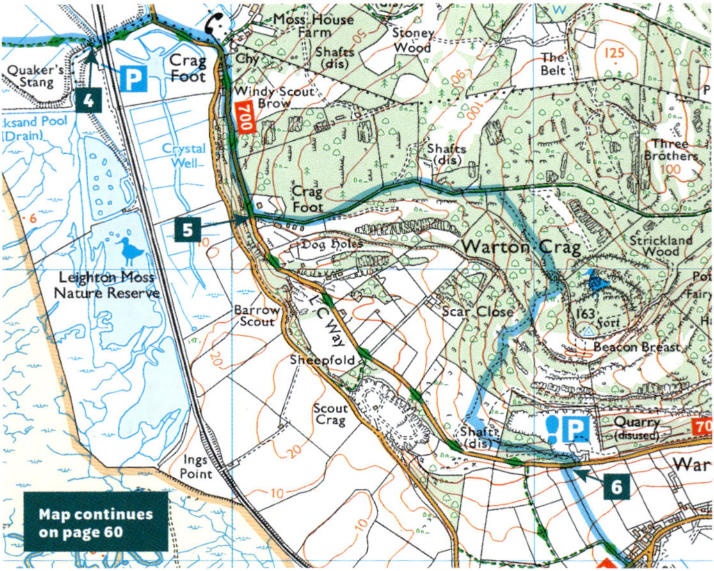

SHORT WALKS IN ARNSIDE AND SILVERDALE

Crag Foot chimney

WALK 9 – SILVERDALE TO CARNFORTH

Descending through farmland towards Carnforth

The chimney at Crag Foot is all that remains of a pumping station, part of a scheme to drain Leighton Moss and improve surrounding agricultural land. The embankment from Heald Brow to Crag Foot was constructed around 1830 to keep back coastal waters.

5 Follow the track until you reach a gate and footpath on the right. Turn right here and proceed uphill through heathland on **Warton Crag** to reach a second gate. Pass through this and fork right, descending to a clearing. Bear left here, picking up the footpath to the quarry car park. Leave the car park onto Crag Road, turn right and walk a short way to find a footpath on your left across a field.

> ⓘ *Warton crag was quarried until 1962 and provided limestone rock used to build the M6 motorway*

6 Follow the path downhill, emerging alongside a house onto the road. Turn right and follow the road as far as a sharp right bend. Continue over a bridge, then turn left to follow a

SHORT WALKS IN ARNSIDE AND SILVERDALE

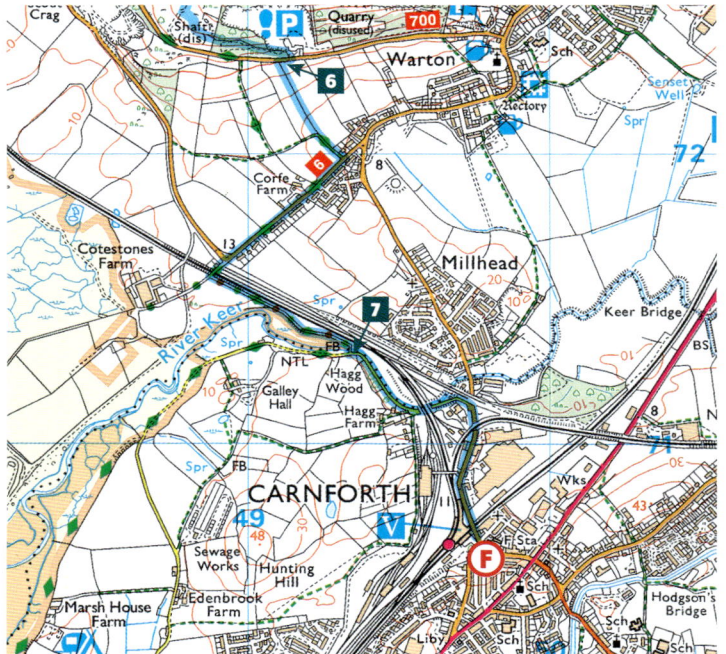

cycleway path to a footbridge over the **River Keer**.

7 Cross this and turn left into a lane. Follow the lane under a railway bridge and then out to the main road. Turn right uphill and around the corner to **Carnforth station**.

Carnforth station was the setting for the classic 1945 film *Brief Encounter*, directed by David Lean and starring Celia Johnson and Trevor Howard. Restored in 2003, the Heritage Centre enables you to experience a little of the era of steam trains and romance.

> **− To shorten**
> Turning back at any point before Crag Foot would make for a shorter out-and-back route.

Footbridge across the River Keer

Finding silver

While it may just be coincidence that the village name of Silverdale hints at the presence of treasure, one of the largest ever Viking hoards in the UK was found here by an amateur metal detectorist. The treasure comprised over 200 pieces of silver and coins of Anglo-Saxon, Viking and Arabic origin, including a coin stamped with the name of a previously unknown Viking ruler. The hoard dates from around AD900, a time of intense conflict between Vikings and Anglo-Saxons in the area.

The chimney at Jenny Brown's Point

WALK 10
Jenny Brown's Point

Start/finish	The Shore, Silverdale
Locate	LA5 0TS ///limitless.latter.trips
Cafes/pubs	Silverdale Hotel pub, Wolf & Us cafe
Transport	Train to Silverdale station, then Bus 51 to village centre
Parking	Shore Road car park
Toilets	In centre of Silverdale (5min off route)

Time: 1¾hr
Distance: 5km (3 miles)
Climb: 120m

With fresh farm ice-cream, an art and craft gallery, the Giant's Seat and coastal views, this moderate walk is one not to be rushed

Stroll along a leafy lane then out onto windswept heathland. The Giant's Seat is a great place to linger and observe the bay, and the tidal bore can be seen developing if your timing is right. There is history to be uncovered as you pick your way over the rocks at Jenny Brown's Point and then pass an intriguing chimney. The climb up Heald Brow towards Hollins Lane is steep but quickly gives way to easier ground as you return through the fascinating Woodwell.

Corner of Hollins Lane near Wolf House Gallery and Gibraltar Farm

SHORT WALKS IN ARNSIDE AND SILVERDALE

1 From the beach, head up Shore Road and around the corner uphill. Take a footpath right, alongside a garage, to emerge onto Lindeth Road.

2 Turn right and walk along this pleasant road to the junction with Hollins Lane. On your left is the Wolf House Gallery and Cafe, and across the junction on your right is Gibraltar Farm & Campsite, famous for its home-made ice-cream. Continue straight ahead along the single-track road, now bordered by trees, passing Lindeth Tower on the right. After a short distance the trees give way to heath and a small gate can be found on your right.

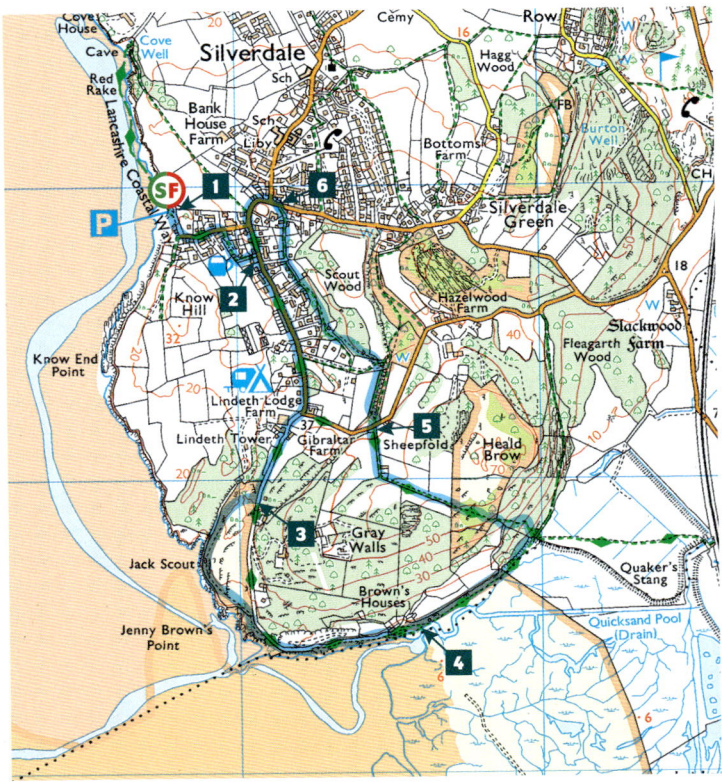

Looking across the estuary to Warton Crag

3 Turn right through the gate and follow the worn path downhill past a well-preserved former limekiln, one of many in this area. Keep ahead through gorse and scrub as the path becomes clearer and guides you around the rocky promontory of **Jack Scout**. In the heath above the path and you will find the Giant's Seat, a rest stop with incredible views that will seat the whole family! Continue around the cliff above the beach, past the small cove at Jenny Brown's Point, then follow the path back out onto the lane. Turn right to reach **Brown's Houses**.

Approaching Brown's Houses

The origin of the name Jenny Brown's Point is unknown. A popular story is that Jenny Brown was a nanny who drowned while trying to rescue children in her care from the incoming tide. All that is known for sure is that two Jenny Browns (mother and daughter) lived at nearby Dykehouse Farm in the mid 17th century.

> ⓘ *Unusual timbers can be spotted out in the saltmarsh at Jenny Brown's Point. These were part of a bombing range used for target practice during WW2*

4 Take the beach path past the tall chimney on the shore then continue on the path along the saltmarsh to a four-way track junction. Turn left,

SHORT WALKS IN ARNSIDE AND SILVERDALE

The pool at Woodwell Cliff

signposted 'Hollins Lane', climbing **Heald Brow** through trees then fields to reach the road.

> Archaeology undertaken in 2017 suggests the chimney was part of a reverberatory furnace built in about 1780 for roasting iron and copper ores, most likely mined from nearby Warton Crag and Heald Brow.

5 Cross the road and turn right then almost immediately left through the wall on a footpath signposted 'Woodwell Cliff'. Keep left and descend to the lower path and follow this to a clearing at Woodwell, where wrought-iron railings surround a pond into which a spring runs from the cliff base. Continue across the small gravel car park and find a footpath into Bottoms Wood. Follow this path on through **Scout Wood** and out to Stankelt Road.

> Rainwater collection and springs such as Woodwell were the primary sources of water for Silverdale. It wasn't until 1938 that a piped supply was arranged by the Lune Valley Water Board.

6 Turn left and follow the road left around the corner, then turn right into Shore Road. Continue downhill and right around the corner to cross the cattle-grid and onto Silverdale shore and car park.

> **+ To lengthen**
>
> Continue beyond the junction in Waypoint 4 for 15min extension through Fleagarth Wood. Turn left past Hazelwood Farm, right through Scout Wood then left along Stankelt Road back to the main route.

WALK 11
Arnside Tower from Silverdale

Start/finish	The Shore, Silverdale
Locate	LA5 0TS ///limitless.latter.trips
Cafes/pubs	The Silverdale Hotel
Transport	Train to Silverdale, then Bus 51 to village centre
Parking	Shore Road car park
Toilets	In centre of Silverdale (5min off route)

Time: 2hr
Distance: 5.5km (3½ miles)
Climb: 110m

A cave, mining remains and a crumbling tower add history and interest to this moderate circular route around Silverdale

Enjoy the coast with its windswept trees and visit a cave on route to historic Arnside Tower, returning through Middlebarrow Plain on good paths to Elmslack and the hidden lanes of Silverdale. Alternatively, start the walk at Arnside Tower and complete the circuit, taking advantage of parking in the layby above the farm.

The beach route to the Cove

SHORT WALKS IN ARNSIDE AND SILVERDALE

1 At low tide the beach route to the Cove is best, but in wet weather or at high tide follow Shore Road uphill, left around the corner and turn left at the junction into Stankelt Road. After 20m or so take the footpath left up steps signposted 'The Cove & Arnside'. Follow this path across the cliff top, through a gate then down into the Cove. The cave in the cliff can be reached from the beach.

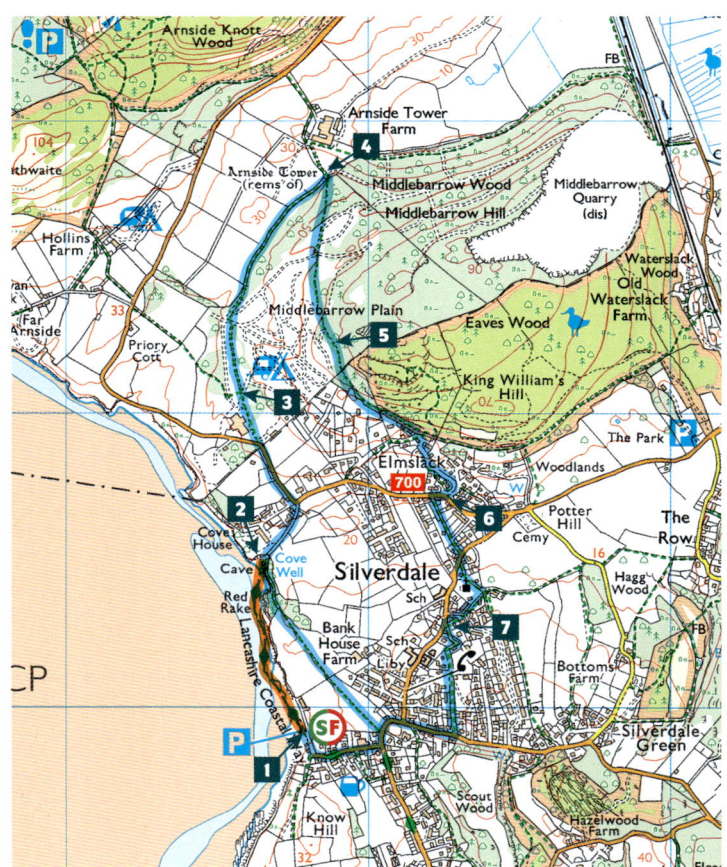

WALK 11 – ARNSIDE TOWER FROM SILVERDALE

The cliff cave

Across from the cave the wooden remains of an old jetty can just be seen protruding from the sand. Behind this was once an old mine where tin and copper ores were extracted, perhaps being roasted at the furnace beyond Jenny Brown's Point.

2 Leave the beach and walk uphill into Cove Road then turn left into Silverdale Road. Follow the stone wall to the bend in the road where you will see a pedestrian gate on the right into Holgates caravan park. Go through this and keep ahead along a footpath. There is a shop on your left if refreshments are needed. Just beyond this the longer option could be taken on a path left signposted 'Far Arnside'.

3 Follow marker posts across the caravan park to a gate under trees. Go through this and follow the good path until you see **Arnside Tower** ahead of you.

> ⓘ *The rivers Kent, Keer and Bela all flow into Morecambe Bay, alongside the Duddon and Leven further west, and the Wyre and Lune further south, creating the largest area of intertidal flats in Britain*

4 Facing Arnside Tower, a second gate is on your right. Go through this and keep right at the fork through scrub and trees, rising to emerge on the caravan site again. Continue in the same direction straight across the site and into the trees on the far side, where a signpost guides you to the path.

5 Continue ahead passing through a stone wall stile and descend gradually to a further wall gap. Go through and follow the path ahead. Emerge from the trees and soon the path becomes a surfaced lane before a fork. Keep right into Castle Lane and continue downhill among houses to the main road.

6 Turn right, past a couple houses, then cross the road and take a footpath left between houses. Follow this to the next road, turn right then almost immediately take a left onto a small track that runs to the rear of the

SHORT WALKS IN ARNSIDE AND SILVERDALE

The cliff-top path to the Cove

church, until you meet an open area and signed track junction. Take the footpath right, signposted 'Emesgate Lane'. Follow this to a junction with St John's Avenue then take the footpath straight ahead between gardens to reach Spring Bank.

7 Turn left into Spring Bank and follow the lane all the way to meet Stankelt Road. Turn right and follow the road left around the corner. Take the right turn into Shore Road then downhill to arrive back at the Shore and the car park.

> **+ To lengthen**
>
> At Waypoint 3 turn left on the footpath across fields, past Hollins Farm, then right through Heathwaite. At the track junction turn right, signposted 'Arnside Tower'. Cross the road, go down the farm lane opposite and around the farm to rejoin the main route at Waypoint 4, adding around 30min.

Arnside Tower

Built in the 15th century from limestone rubble, the five-storey tower had an adjacent wing, a style usually only seen in Scotland. Tower houses such as this were built to protect against the threat from 'Border Reivers', raiders and bandits that exploited the border and disputed areas. Badly burned in a fire in 1602, Arnside Tower was repaired and occupied again, but later partially dismantled for materials. It was almost split in two in a storm in 1884. The interior is in a poor state and it is not recommended to enter the ruins.

The south-west corner of the Arnside Tower collapsed in a storm in 1884

The route follows tracks and paths through mixed woodland

WALK 12
The Pepperpot and Eaves Wood

Start/finish	*Eaves Wood car park*
Locate	*LA5 0QU ///handbook.pigtails.mopped*
Cafes/pubs	*None on route*
Transport	*Take Park Road from Silverdale. Bus 51 to The Row. Train to Silverdale station then 15min walk along busy lane*
Parking	*National Trust car park at Eaves Wood (free)*
Toilets	*No public toilets available*

Time: 1½hr
Distance: 3km (1¾ miles)
Climb: 90m

A moderate stroll through coppiced woodland rich in wildlife, and a couple of interesting historic monuments

Eaves Wood contains arguably some of the best ancient woodland in the country. Rich in wildlife and ancient folklore, this circular walk rewards the walker at the summit with an unusual landmark and outstanding views, but the keen-eyed will find much to see along the route too. Tracks are good, but for much of the walk it is limestone under foot so care is required after rain, as it is slippery when wet.

Evening sun lends a magical feel to the wood

SHORT WALKS IN ARNSIDE AND SILVERDALE

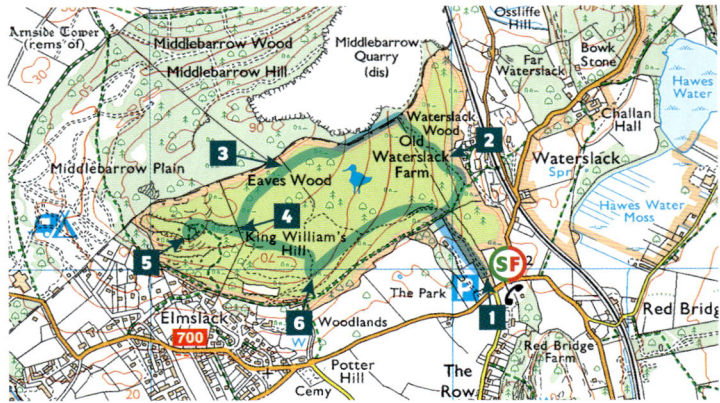

1 Leave the car park uphill via a gate and climb gently to a junction. Turn right and follow the sign to Waterslack. Pass stone posts on the left where a gate once stood and keep straight ahead to cross a boundary wall, then descend slightly and keep left. Ignore a side path right, but keep ahead for a further 150m until the path forks by a large oak tree with a smaller yew nestling under its boughs.

2 Take the smaller path left uphill. Keep right at the next fork and stay parallel to the stone boundary wall until you reach a step-through, where you cross over and continue uphill. After a few minutes bear slightly right, stepping up onto limestone pavement through pine trees. Keep left on the limestone shortly before the next boundary wall, and then straight ahead parallel with the wall. Continue to a gate in a stone wall under a yew tree.

3 Proceed through the gate and ahead across a track junction, then on through an airy copse, on limestone once more. After some way the path descends into tree cover, past intriguing hexagonal stone remains on the left, under twisted old yew trees, and then down bordered stone steps to a gate, all of which lends a mythical feel.

> **The hexagonal remains (and the name 'King William's Hill') are believed to originate from around 1830, when a gazebo and steps were built to commemorate King William IV's accession to the throne.**

All that remains of King William IV's monument from 1830

SHORT WALKS IN ARNSIDE AND SILVERDALE

The Pepperpot, with views over Silverdale and the bay

Emes Cottage, believed to have been a gamekeeper's home

WALK 12 – THE PEPPERPOT AND EAVES WOOD

> ⓘ Among the features of the AONB are the 'glacial erratics', boulders typically from the central Lake District, carried here by glaciers during the last ice age

4 Go through the gate and turn right through a gap in the wall onto a clear broad track. Pass on through a clearing to a fork in the path, bearing left uphill signposted 'Pepperpot'. Carefully climb the stony path to emerge on the plateau of Castlebarrow, one summit of King William's Hill. The Pepperpot is now ahead of you.

Emes Cottage now provides a home for moss, lichen and ferns

> Built around 1887 to mark the Golden Jubilee of Queen Victoria, the monument (known locally as The Pepperpot) was commissioned by the Hebden family, who owned Castlebarrow. Views extend across Morecambe Bay, even as far as Blackpool Tower on a really clear day.

5 Carefully retrace your steps for it is easy to become disoriented as numerous tracks surround the summit. Continue past the signed track junction, across the clearing and through the boundary wall, then bear right downhill following a sign for the car park and turn right at a junction following waymarks. The path weaves downhill to reach a signposted track junction.

6 Take the left path, signposted 'The Beech Circle', which is reached after a couple of minutes. The origins of the Beech Circle remain a mystery, but locally it is sometimes referred to as the Fairy Circle. Continue past the remains of Emes Cottage (built around 1808). Descending further, pass under oak and yew, and a limestone crag on your left leads to the track junction marked by two ancient stone 'gate posts'. Turn right and retrace your steps to the car park.

> **– To shorten**
>
> Turn left at the track junction at Waypoint 3 and descend to the lower path where a further left leads you back to the car park.

Arnside Tower dominates the skyline

WALK 13
Middlebarrow Wood and Eaves Wood

Start/finish	*Eaves Wood car park*
Locate	*LA5 0QU ///handbook.pigtails.mopped*
Cafes/pubs	*None on route*
Transport	*Take Park Road from Silverdale. Bus 51 to The Row. Train to Silverdale station then 15min walk along busy lane*
Parking	*National Trust car park at Eaves Wood (free)*
Toilets	*No public toilets available*

Time: 2¼hr
Distance: 4.5km (2¾ miles)
Climb: 135m

Arnside Tower is the highlight of this delightful, easy walk through woodland, wildlife, farmland and history

Good tracks make easy walking through Eaves Wood and the quieter Middlebarrow Wood, and the keen-eyed will be rewarded with glimpses of wildlife. This is undoubtedly the most dramatic approach to Arnside Tower. The route could be completed starting and finishing at Arnside Tower, using the parking in the layby above the farm.

Eaves Wood is home to some fabulous old trees

SHORT WALKS IN ARNSIDE AND SILVERDALE

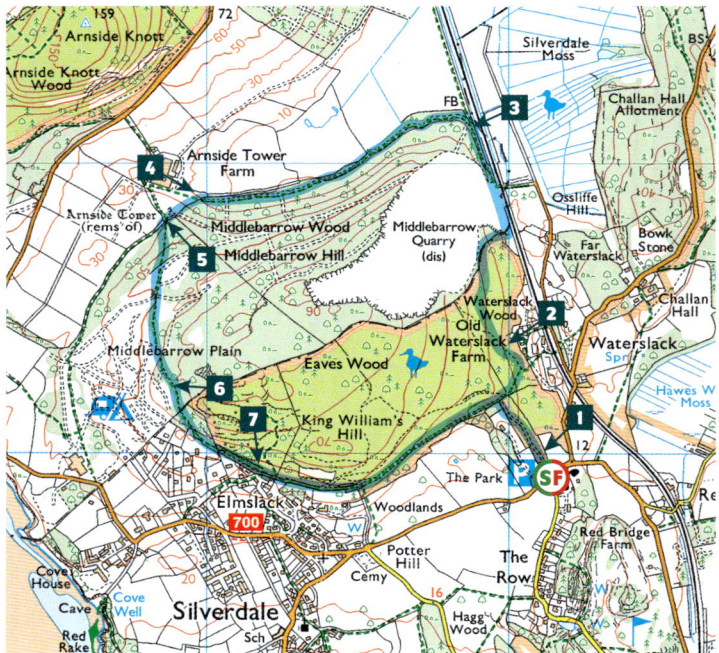

1 Leave the car park uphill via a gate and climb gently to a junction. Turn right and follow the sign to Waterslack. Pass stone posts on the left where a gate once stood and keep ahead to cross a boundary wall, then descend slightly and keep left. Ignoring a side path keep ahead for 150m until the path forks by a large oak tree with a smaller yew nestling under its boughs.

2 Keep right here and proceed ahead under the boughs of another large old oak tree. The path weaves through close woodland until a stone boundary wall is reached. Pass through this, turning sharply right, following 'concessionary path' marker posts downhill. Take care on the limestone here if it's wet. Bear left on this path alongside the railway tracks, past the entrance to the now disused **Middlebarrow Quarry**. Continue through quiet shady woodland to reach a fork in the path.

WALK 13 – MIDDLEBARROW WOOD AND EAVES WOOD

Looking across Arnside Tower Farm towards Arnside Knott

3 Take the left fork signposted to Arnside Tower and follow the path through the back of **Middlebarrow Wood**, where deer regularly graze. Continue until you reach a gate at the boundary of the wood and Arnside Tower Farm.

> ⓘ *Buildings and settlements constructed from local limestone, dating back to medieval times around 800 years ago, are scattered throughout the AONB*

4 Pass through the gate and out onto the stony farm hillside. Turn left for the short climb to **Arnside Tower**.

Built as a freestanding tower rather than attached to other buildings, Arnside Tower is an almost unique example of a Cumbrian pele tower. Originally five storeys tall, fire, storm and dismantling have left a ruin almost split in two.

Arnside Tower was built in the 15th century

5 Continuing uphill, if the stile on your left remains in disrepair, pass through the wall gap ahead, then immediately left through the gate. Keep right as the path forks and ascend through scrub and trees to emerge into Holgates caravan park. Yellow footpath arrows guide you straight across and back into the trees on the far side.

6 Continue ahead, passing through a stone wall stile, and descend gradually to a further wall gap where the path proceeds clearly ahead. Shortly afterwards you will emerge from the trees and the path becomes a surfaced lane before it forks.

7 Keep left at the fork. Continue ahead into **Eaves Wood**, keeping the boundary wall on your right. Ignoring side paths, proceed with glimpses across the fields to your right until you reach the signpost marking the avenue back to the car park. Turn right and retrace your outward route down the track to the start.

Looking back towards Elmslack on the return journey through Eaves Wood

WALK 14
Arnside to Silverdale

Start	*Arnside railway station*
Locate	*LA7 0HG ///both.sharpness.metals*
Finish	*Silverdale railway station*
Cafes/pubs	*Pubs and cafes in Arnside, cafe at RSPB Leighton Moss, Silverdale*
Transport	*Trains to/from Arnside and Silverdale*
Parking	*Roadside or car parking in Arnside*
Toilets	*On Arnside promenade*

Time: 2¾hr
Distance: 7km (4¼ miles)
Climb: 185m

A linear walk from Arnside's busy promenade, through quieter woodland, hills and fields, exploring the lanes of Silverdale to return by train

This linear route offers the opportunity to see much of the richness and variety of the AONB landscapes in just one walk. Combining more popular routes with less walked paths and lanes enables the walker to get to know the area better. The relaxing return by train offers views over Silverdale Moss that are not otherwise easily seen.

Arnside station with the signal box beyond, a listed building in its own right

SHORT WALKS IN ARNSIDE AND SILVERDALE

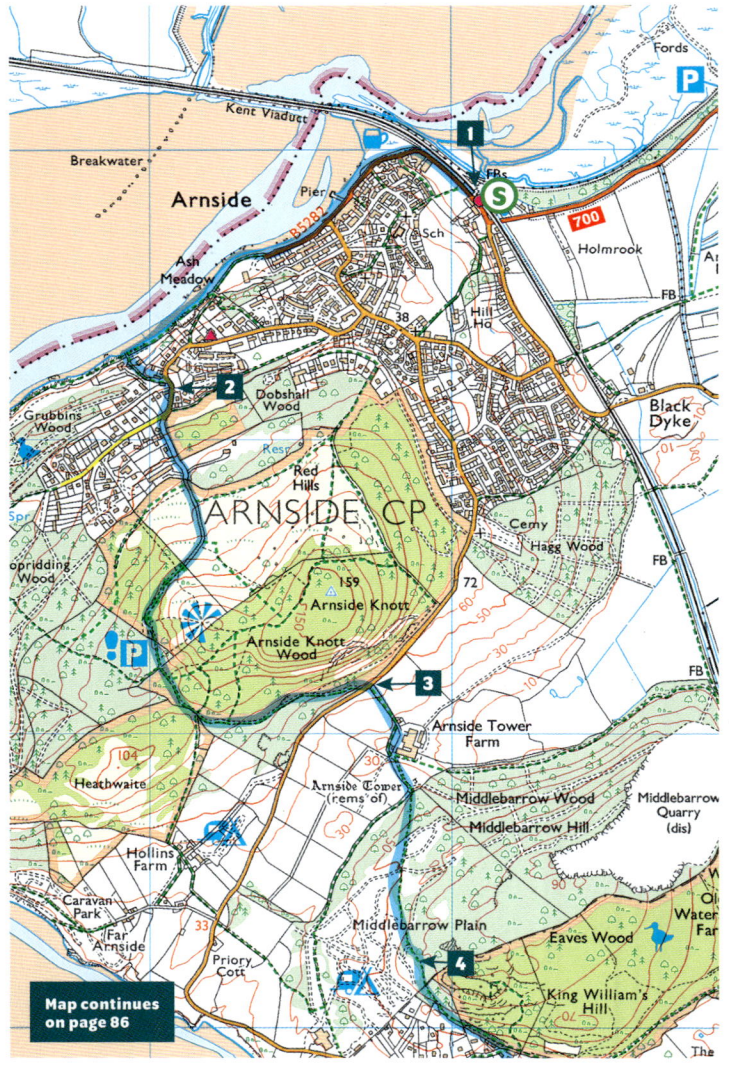

WALK 14 — ARNSIDE TO SILVERDALE

Emerging onto Red Hills Road by the Coach House

1 Turn right from **Arnside station** and follow the promenade round past the pier, beyond the shops. Keep right past Ashmeadow House. Continue past the coastguard hut and on towards the prominent flagpole visible ahead. Just before this, a slipway leads left uphill. Take this, emerging onto Red Hills Road by the old coach house.

2 Turn right, past **Dobshall Wood** to a lane signposted 'The Knott'. Take this left, steeply uphill. Eventually cross a cattle-grid and continue towards the gravel car park. Keep left of the parking space on a broad track, initially through two gates, then through a third gate signposted to Arnside Tower, and descend through dappled woodland to the road.

3 At the road cross to descend the farm lane, towards Arnside Tower. Take the footpath right around the farm edge, then climb, passing the tower on your left, to a large wooden stile. If the stile remains in disrepair, pass through the wall gap to the right, then immediately left through the gate. Keep right at a fork to ascend through scrub and trees into Holgates

The track up to the Knott car park

SHORT WALKS IN ARNSIDE AND SILVERDALE

Arnside Tower Farm seen from further up Silverdale Road

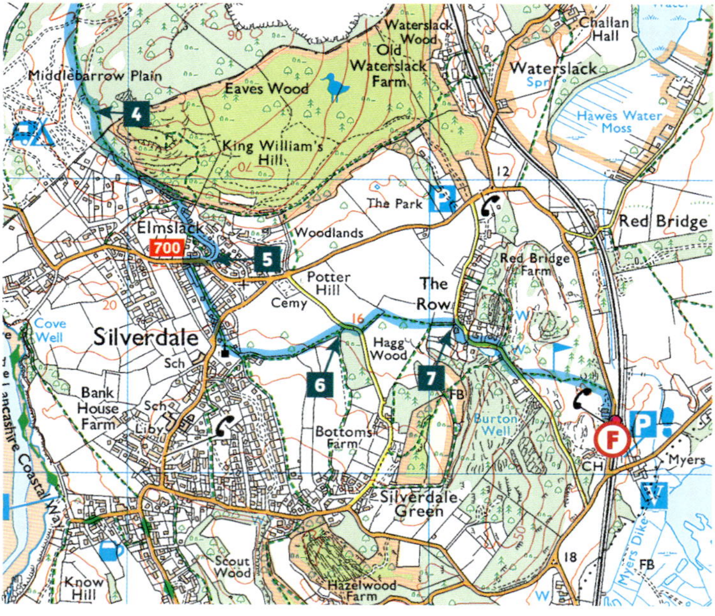

WALK 14 — ARNSIDE TO SILVERDALE

caravan park. Yellow footpath arrows guide you straight across and into the trees on the far side.

4 Continue ahead through a stone wall stile and descend to a further gap in a boundary wall and proceed through. The track becomes a surfaced lane, then forks. Keep right into Castle Lane and continue downhill among houses.

5 At the main road turn right, past a couple of houses, then take a footpath left between houses. Follow this to the next road, turn right then almost immediately take a left onto a small track that runs to the rear of the church, until you meet an open area and signed track junction. Take the left footpath here, signposted 'Bottoms Lane', behind gardens then along field boundaries to a road.

6 Cross and turn right for 50m then left into a field signposted 'The Row'. Pass through a wall gap on your right and across two more fields before reaching a lane and cottages, and a sign for the station.

7 Turn right, uphill initially, past a reed bed on your right, then take a footpath left across the **golf course**, signposted 'Silverdale station'. Cross two fairways and exit through a break in the wall to the road. Turn right and **Silverdale station** is ahead on your left.

The Furness branch line connects Lancaster with Barrow-in-Furness, travelling along the coast to Carnforth, then weaving its way past Silverdale and Arnside, before crossing the viaduct to Grange and on to Ulverston and Barrow. This scenic route enables spectacular views across Leighton Moss and Silverdale Moss as well as the estuary.

Footpath behind houses signposted Bottoms Lane

Levens Park's famous avenue of oak trees

WALK 15
Levens Park and the River Kent

Time: 1¾hr
Distance: 4.5km (2¾ miles)
Climb: 100m

Ancient trees, the flowing river and rare-breed goats are highlights of this peaceful, historic park

Start/finish	*Levens Bridge*
Locate	*LA8 0PD ///coining.dumps.cautious*
Cafes/pubs	*Cafe at Levens Hall*
Transport	*Take A6 from Milnthorpe. Bus 99 or 555*
Parking	*Layby on old A6 beyond Levens Hall*
Toilets	*No public toilets available*

While just outside of the AONB, this walk is not to be missed. Some truly ancient trees border the winding River Kent through lovely parkland that shelters a herd of deer and rare-breed goats grazing along an avenue of oaks.

The River Kent flows peacefully through Levens Park

SHORT WALKS IN ARNSIDE AND SILVERDALE

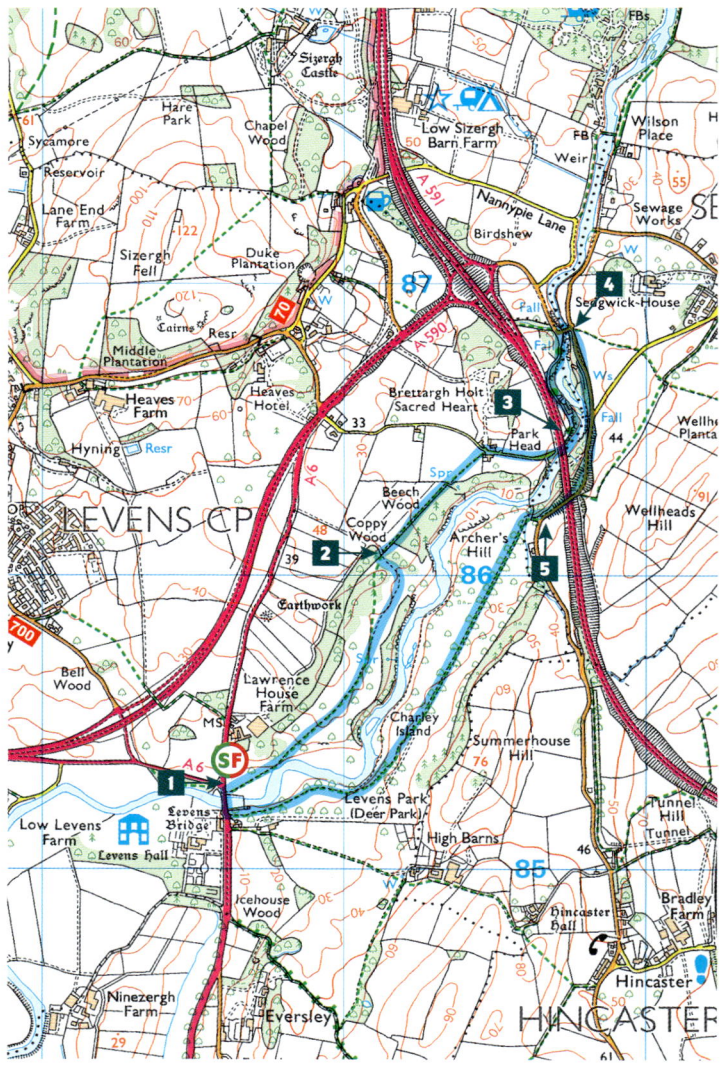

WALK 15 – LEVENS PARK AND THE RIVER KENT

Twelve generations of a family could have passed under this 17th-century tree

1 Take the swing gate left through a wall gap on the old stone bridge. Keep the river to your right and follow the worn path. Marker posts guide you as you climb gently above the river. Continue through meadow, turning away from the river, to reach steps over a stone wall, nestled under a chestnut tree.

> **The older trees in the park were planted between 1689 and 1712 by French gardener Guillaume Beaumont, the gardener of King James II and the designer of the grounds at Hampton Court Palace.**

2 Here you leave the park for a way, contour around its northern perimeter and cross the river. Cross the wall via the steps and turn right, then keeping the wall on your right, follow it across two fields to a stile. Cross this and turn right, descending the lane between cottages at **Park Head**. The lane narrows to a path and here go down steps under the main A591 road to reveal a surprisingly tranquil stretch of river.

3 Keep ahead on a leafy lane for a few minutes to reach a road junction and bridge. Turn right and cross the river.

The Grade II listed Levens Bridge dates from the 17th century

4 Across the bridge turn right again, along a lane signposted 'Hincaster'. Cross back over the main road and descend a short way to a gate into **Levens Park** once more.

5 A carved stone seat ahead of you overlooks a tranquil section of the river and park, where deer can often be seen grazing. Take the path left, along the avenue of oaks. As you near the end of the avenue, the path forks. Keep right where a helpful arrow guides you and descend towards the river. Reaching a stile in the wall by the bridge, pass through and turn right to return to the layby, or cross the road to visit Levens Hall and cafe.

The rare Bagot goat is one of Britain's oldest breeds

WALK 15 – LEVENS PARK AND THE RIVER KENT

✚ To lengthen

Just before Waypoint 4 continue ahead without crossing the bridge. Turn right on Nannypie Lane and follow the river to explore the Old Sedgwick Gunpowder Works. At the Low Wood Suspension Bridge, cross the river, turn right, and return on the opposite bank.

Levens Hall

Levens Hall is a privately owned Elizabethan house built around a 13th-century pele tower. It has a fascinating history, including being gambled and lost in a game of cards in the 17th century. It is perhaps now most famous for having the world's oldest topiary garden, dating to 1690. The house and gardens are open Sun–Thurs, April to October and the recently developed Levens Kitchen which opened in 2019 has already won awards for its locally sourced, high-quality produce, including products grown on the estate. The Kitchen is open seven days a week between 10am and 4pm (www.levenshall.co.uk).

Historic Levens Hall

USEFUL INFORMATION

Trains

The Furness line between Barrow and Lancaster serves Carnforth, Silverdale and Arnside. It connects to the West Coast Mainline at Lancaster and there is a direct service to Manchester and the airport. To find out what else is along the Furness line visit:

www.communityrailcumbria.co.uk/lines/furness-line/

Trainline

www.thetrainline.com

Northern

www.northernrailway.co.uk

Buses

For bus timetables and information visit

www.stagecoachbus.com/about/cumbria-and-north-lancashire.

The most useful bus services for walks in this guide are:

- 99 connecting Arnside with Kendal and stops at Levens Hall (school days and times only)
- 555 connecting Lancaster and Carnforth with Milnthorpe, Levens Hall, Kendal and beyond to Keswick (7 days a week)
- 51 connecting Carnforth with Warton, Silverdale and Holgates Caravan Park (6 days a week)

© David Jordan 2023
First edition 2023
ISBN: 978 1 78631 158 0

Printed in India by Replika Press Pvt Ltd using responsibly sourced paper.
A catalogue record for this book is available from the British Library.

© Crown copyright 2023 OS PU100012932
All photographs are by the author unless otherwise stated.

CICERONE

Cicerone Press, Juniper House, Murley Moss, Oxenholme Road, Kendal, Cumbria, LA9 7RL

www.cicerone.co.uk

Updates to this Guide

While every effort is made to ensure the accuracy of guidebooks as they go to print, changes can occur during the lifetime of an edition. Any updates that we know of for this guide will be on the Cicerone website (www.cicerone.co.uk/1158/updates), so please check before planning your trip. We also advise that you check information about transport, accommodation and shops locally. We are always grateful for updates, sent by email to updates@cicerone.co.uk or by post to Cicerone, Juniper House, Murley Moss, Oxenholme Road, Kendal, LA9 7RL.

Register your book: To sign up to receive free updates, special offers and GPX files where available, register your book at www.cicerone.co.uk.

Tourism and nature organisations

Arnside and Silverdale Area of Outstanding Natural Beauty
www.arnsidesilverdaleaonb.org.uk
The National Trust
www.nationaltrust.org.uk/arnside-and-silverdale
RSPB
www.rspb.org.uk
Arnside village website
http://arnsidevillage.co.uk/

Further reading

For a brief history of the fascinating area beyond Levens Park (Walk 15), see
www.sedgwickparishcouncil.org.uk/a-detailed-history---part-2--the-wake-fields-gunpowder-era-in-sedgwick.html
For more on features of particular geological interest included on the Storth Geotrail (Walk 4) visit
www.arnsidesilverdaleaonb.org.uk/uploads/2016/04/storth_geotrail.pdf
For more about the history of Ashmeadow see
www.barnescharitabletrust.org.uk/?HISTORY